HAL•LEONARD
INSTRUMENTAL PLAY-ALONG

TRUMPET

Disney Classics

THE CD IS PLAYABLE ON ANY CD PLAYER. FOR PC AND MAC USERS, THE CD IS ENHANCED SO YOU CAN ADJUST THE RECORDING TO ANY TEMPO WITHOUT CHANGING PITCH.

The following songs are the property of:
BOURNE CO.
Music Publishers
5 West 37th Street
New York, NY 10018

Baby Mine	Some Day My Prince Will Come
Give a Little Whistle	When You Wish Upon a Star
Heigh-Ho	Whistle While You Work
I've Got No Strings	Who's Afraid of the Big Bad Wolf?

ISBN 978-1-4584-1600-1

WALT DISNEY MUSIC COMPANY
WONDERLAND MUSIC COMPANY, INC.

DISTRIBUTED BY

7777 W. BLUEMOUND RD. P.O. BOX 13819 MILWAUKEE, WI 53213

Visit Hal Leonard Online at
www.halleonard.com

ALICE IN WONDERLAND

from Walt Disney's ALICE IN WONDERLAND

Words by BOB HILLIARD
Music by SAMMY FAIN

TRUMPET

1/2

BABY MINE

from Walt Disney's DUMBO

Words by NED WASHINGTON
Music by FRANK CHURCHILL

TRUMPET

Slowly, with feeling

BELLA NOTTE
(This Is the Night)
from Walt Disney's LADY AND THE TRAMP

Words and Music by PEGGY LEE
and SONNY BURKE

TRUMPET

GIVE A LITTLE WHISTLE

from Walt Disney's PINOCCHIO

7/8

TRUMPET

Words by NED WASHINGTON
Music by LEIGH HARLINE

HEIGH-HO

The Dwarfs' Marching Song from Walt Disney's SNOW WHITE AND THE SEVEN DWARFS

Words by LARRY MOREY
Music by FRANK CHURCHILL

9/10
TRUMPET

I'VE GOT NO STRINGS

from Walt Disney's PINOCCHIO

Words by NED WASHINGTON
Music by LEIGH HARLINE

TRUMPET

LITTLE APRIL SHOWER

from Walt Disney's BAMBI

Words by LARRY MOREY
Music by FRANK CHURCHILL

TRUMPET

Playfully

ONCE UPON A DREAM

from Walt Disney's SLEEPING BEAUTY

15/16

TRUMPET

Words and Music by SAMMY FAIN
and JACK LAWRENCE
Adapted from a Theme by Tchaikovsky

SOME DAY MY PRINCE WILL COME

from Walt Disney's SNOW WHITE AND THE SEVEN DWARFS

Words by LARRY MOREY
Music by FRANK CHURCHILL

17/18

TRUMPET

THE UNBIRTHDAY SONG
from Walt Disney's ALICE IN WONDERLAND

19/20

TRUMPET

Words and Music by MACK DAVID,
AL HOFFMAN and JERRY LIVINGSTON

WHEN YOU WISH UPON A STAR

from Walt Disney's PINOCCHIO

21/22

TRUMPET

Words by NED WASHINGTON
Music by LEIGH HARLINE

WHISTLE WHILE YOU WORK

from Walt Disney's SNOW WHITE AND THE SEVEN DWARFS

23/24

TRUMPET

Words by LARRY MOREY
Music by FRANK CHURCHILL

WHO'S AFRAID OF THE BIG BAD WOLF?

from Walt Disney's THREE LITTLE PIGS

25/26

TRUMPET

Words and Music by FRANK CHURCHILL
Additional Lyric by ANN RONELL

YOU CAN FLY! YOU CAN FLY! YOU CAN FLY!

from Walt Disney's PETER PAN

Words by SAMMY CAHN
Music by SAMMY FAIN

27/28

TRUMPET